FROM VOLYN

TO KHERSON

INTERPRETATIONS
OF THE WAR
IN UKRAINE

FRANK PREM

Publication Details

Title: *From Volyn To Kherson*
ISBN: 978-1-925963-83-0 (p-bk)
ISBN: 978-1-925963-86-1 (e-bk)

Published by Wild Arancini Press
2022

All rights reserved:
No part of this publication may be reproduced, stored in a retrieval system, or transmitted in any form or by any means, electronic, mechanical, photocopying, recording or otherwise, without prior written permission from the publisher and author.

Which of us will be Ukraine, tomorrow?

Contents

About *From Volyn To Kherson*	1
From Volyn To Kherson	5
Sources	159
Author Information	165
Other Published Works	169
What Readers Say	173
Index of Individual Poems	177

About *From Volyn To Kherson*

From Volyn To Kherson is a poetry collection drawn from the news of the day, beginning in February of 2022, when Russia invaded Ukraine in a war without declaration.

The stories told here were first told by reporters and their news agencies. By *The BBC* of Britain and *The ABC* of Australia. T*he Guardian Newspaper* and *The Washington Post*.

They were told by individuals on social media such as Twitter and Facebook.

The poems come from Volyn, located on the Polish border with Ukraine and from Kherson near the Crimea and The Sea of Azov.

From Zmiinyi Island in the Black sea and from Kyiv.

There is no part of Ukraine that has been left untouched by stories of war, and no part of this poet left untouched by these stories of the Ukraine.

Sources for each poem are referenced at the back of the book.

This collection is a companion volume to B*ullets Into The Starichi Sky*, and *I Call The Hole The War* (both unreleased) which interpreted the images taken by photographers on the ground in Ukraine through the first nine weeks of the conflict.

FP
June 2022

From Volyn To Kherson

a lullaby (for lviv)

rocket trails
are hanging
in the sky

stars in motion
over lviv

night is day
and day
is noise
all through
the shelter hours

sirens sound

missiles strike

women cry

and then
they line up
to receive
a rifle

birth happens
in
bomb shelters

children
find Poland
but not
their parents

a man of passion
kneels
on the road
in front of a tank

this is
a pleading
war

a vision
of resistance

the dying
is off screen
(so far)

invaders wonder
where they are

is this
the road to
there

is this the road
to anywhere
at all

a grandma
has cleared
the table
in her kitchen

ingredients
are spread around
as though
to make a cake
or maybe
biscuits
or easter bread

but not this time

a green-glass
bottle

a little
motor oil

the vodka she distilled
from theblue plums
last year

and then
some wicking

ten have been made
so far

there will be fifteen more
from this amount
of spirit

it is not
much

it is
everything

it is
something
to say that she loves
her home

her ukraine

that she knows
who is
right
and who
is wrong

as surely
as god knows
to make the sun rise up
over lviv
again
in the morning

the song she hums
underneath
her breath
is
a lullaby

right now (we are kyiv)

right now
we have electricity

right now
we have water

and heating

right now . . .

kyiv
is surrounded
right now

there is no way
for any of us
to leave
and

we are ensuring –
by every means –
there is no
way
to enter

we are –
right now –
all there is
of kyiv

and we hold –
right now –
all there is
of kyiv

it is shrinking –
that is true –
as we are
constricted
and
constrained –

but
right now
we have . . .

we are

all
that there is
of kyiv

anastasia and tatiana (moscva is too close)

*you can be
arrested*

*you can be
put
in prison*

*the policemen
do not care*

*they
can beat you*

*moscva is
too close
to home*

*they do not ask
if war
is right*

*do not ask if
this war
is right*

*they hear
through blunted
batons*

*and take us
away*

*this is not
our war*

says anastasia

> *the dictator
> must fall*

says tatiana

> *if not
> today . . .*
>
> *maybe
> tomorrow*
>
> *I hope
> there will be
> a tomorrow*
>
> *we might be
> in gaol*

holding vlado (close)

kiss me
vlado

I want you
close

hold me
vlado
I need you . . .

close

bite
your tongue

stab
your heart

whisper
goodbye
as you go

kiss me
vlado
I want you . . .

really

close

back into the (snake) water

there are snakes
threatening
zmiinyi island

do not
be fooled
by the name

the asps
are out
on the water –
coming in –

threatening
the zmiinyi
island

but
if words
will do –
and I know
they will not –
those vipers
can bite themselves
right back
into
snake water

fallen (quietly weeping)

my friends
are weeping

quietly

what can be
said
or done
from here . . .

so far

here it is safe

safe enough
to shed
a tear

one drop
for every time
they fire
a gun

now allies
and idiots
are joining the war

conquest –
of a kind –
will draw them
in

another gun

another bomb

perhaps
the nuclear option . . .

what for?

do you know?

is there
a reason
you can find?

what for?

another tear
is
all the good
there ever was

falling into
a little dust
that has been left
behind

and I can't help
but
to believe
that you
and I
and
all of us
and
all the good
there ever was
have fallen

the blue and yellow blood (of the deputy mayor of kakhovka)

in kakhovka
the deputy mayor
is posting pictures
of war wounds

he believed
this
was a last form
of goodbye

they saved him
though

that world
is full of heroes
of all kinds

kharkiv and kyiv
are getting blasted

reporters say
the ground shakes
as though
a live thing

invasion
takes no heed
of what

or who
or how

or
why

~

one inch
one foot
one yard –
call it
a meter –
will do

one foot

another yard

another metre

destroy it
as you go

make sure
that it
all
goes up in smoke

black and grey
and brown

make sure

~

in kakhovka
the deputy mayor
is still alive
you know

for a second

for
a minute

call it
another hour

his heart
is beating
blue
and yellow
blood

the metro (is also home)

seventeen miles
of convoy
stretches out
on the road
to kyiv

the air raid sirens
fill the streets

foreboding

they come
relentlessly

they come
despite

they are
so many
and they come . . .

~

in the shelter
of a railway station
a sole trumpeter
blows

people
sheltered there –
for protection
when the missiles strike –
stand up tall

let the fear
fall away
for a moment while
the anthem
sounds

filling up
the space

with the belief
that even this
is home

vasylkiv (is fighting on)

my secretary
is just nineteen
but
she almost lives here
now

twenty-four
seven

she
is an angry girl

not afraid
of these
invaders

maybe
that will come
but
right now . . .

she
is fearless

I am the mayor
of vasylkiv
we are
a little way
from kyiv

we have
an airfield
that attracts the war

like flies
they buzz

but
the accountant –
from my city office –
is
a mild man

he is commanding –
now –
our territorial defences

do you know
they have struck
our schools

left holes in that space
behind them

and we –
a few of us –
are sheltering
in a cellar

we are religious
you know
ukranians believe
in god

and we video-called
our priest

all of us prayed
together

we each
said our words
to god

as the walls shook
I thought
that I . . .

thought
that I might die

right in
that moment

but –
so far –
we are fighting
on

tell the world that
vasylkiv
is wearing flak jackets
now
and it is fighting
on

> *"People used to think about new car or iPhone, but nobody was thinking about peace. Now, we are dreaming of it. When old people used to wish each other peace, we didn't understand what they meant. Now we do."*

god knows (volyn and rivne)

air raid sirens
are sounding
in rivne

they can hear them
too
in ternopil

and volyn

how long
did it take –
I wonder –
to build
so many airplanes

to attack so many
towns
all at once

I suppose
the next
will be lutsk
although
god knows
what she has done
to cause offence

god knows
what
any of them
have done

in okhtyrka (the tsentral'ne)

they are preparing
the cemetery now
in okhtyrka

andriy
and his platoon
are gone

vacuum bombed

air taken
out
of them

and then
they died

~

in okhtyrka
they are digging

grave
on grave

I think
the cemetery
is
the tsentral'ne

or
the tsvyntar

it doesn't matter
which

there won't be
any funerals held
for awhile

and both of them
will be overrun
before
too long

tears in the storm-water system (are kharkiv's blood)

it is three-thirty
ay-em

the enemy
has found a way
into
kharkiv

and that way
is by missile
and
by bomb

it is
by way
of residential streets
and houses

by schools
and hospitals
and kindergartens

there is blood
filling the drains
like
storm-water

running away
like tears

fallen
like rain

the glory (of the national digital library of ukraine)

We know that no Librarian and no Library are sitting with their hands folded today!

Ukrainian Library Association (Day 6)

someone
is collecting food
and medicine

someone
is turning their library
into a hostel

providing
a little heating
a little food

helping mothers
with
their little children . . .

who
have to go
to another country

to safety

someone
is giving blood
to save
a life

the rest of us
are saving books
from rockets

or
helping territorial
defences

some
of us
are simply
speaking *true things*
where we can –

unanswered lies
are such a powerful
weapon

we know
that we will
win
this war

and
when we do
we will turn all
the knowledge
that we hold
within our paper books
into e-pub

and send
all we know
around the world

oh
what glory
the national digital library
of ukraine
will then be

ants with one heart (one home)

*we
are the ants
of lviv
you know*

*just little ants
but
we are many*

*and we are
as one
in what we do*

*a long time
ago –
one week –
I was working
behind
a desk*

*now
I will make
history*

vitali
had never held
a weapon
before the two weeks
just past

now he wields
a gun

his work colleague
does first-aid

his grandmother
is making bombs
and
urging

this is a fight
for home and
for the heart

vitali says

> we don't
> negotiate
> with terrorists
>
> we are an army
> of ants
> you know
>
> we think –
> we act –
> like creatures
> with the same
> mind
>
> the same
> heart
>
> and only
> one home

o oleg (kherson is falling)

o oleg

o
o

your papa –
oleg *one* –
and your mama
anna
o

o
o o

irina

sophia
and little ivan

o o

kherson is falling
o
o o

one family –
one oleg –
at a time

and I have no words
to say
what I feel

but o

o oleg
o

moscow children (are very very wise)

in moscow
the children
wish to say
no
to war

in moscow
policemen
are
interested

the words
of little children
are sometimes
very wise

and
even a policeman
may listen
to advice

listen –
for fresh wisdom –
to your children

kyiv gives birth (in its basements)

alina
is in the basement

that's where
they deliver children
now
in kyiv hospitals

upstairs
the maternity ward
is taking bullets
and shells

but
babies
must be born

and the basement
is deep

safer than above
where the explosions
made new mothers
scream

the question
that remains –
of course –
is where to go to
next

when the babies
are born
but the missiles
are landing closer

take another tank (for the motherland)

there is no
tax
on a second-hand
tank
in ukraine

the authorities there
say
you can commandeer
as many
as you want

keep them

use them
to plough
the fields

drive them
to church
on a sunday

it is
allowable
they say
because
of cost

one tank
is not worth
one hundred living
wages

so keep it

use it

and if you get
the chance. . .

why

if you get the chance
take
another

a search for solace (for a champion)

the piano man
of taksim square
has moved
to poland

solace
from the piano
for the weary
on the border

so many
saddened souls

so many
weary feet
and legs
and bodies

so many
so tired
they cannot
think

so . . .

he plays for them
again

~

a young woman
has just arrived
across the border line

she has not slept
for days
and almost cannot
begin again
her weeping

but she takes
a place
at the keyboard

starts
to play . . .

> *we*
> *are the champions*
> *my friend*
>
> *we'll*
> *keep on fighting*
> *to the end . . .*

an old
anthem
by the pop group
queen

she finishes
her rendition

rises

walks away
in search
of an elusive
moment
of peace

there will be a party soon (in the kyiv forest)

*welcome
to our party*

men
are digging trenches

planting
tank traps

camouflaging
the forest

young soldiers
boys and girls
still
are being trained
in five minute
warfare

five second
first-aid

to save a limb

save
a life

all of them
are something
that
they *used to be*

but *are not*
any more

they are soldiers
waiting
for the festivities
to begin

after maxim's five liters (say goodbye)

I filled the bath
with water
before
they cut off
the supply

we have nothing
in the taps
and mariupol
has had no power
for two days
now

there is no
food
to be had
anymore

I am living
in the hallway
with my old people
now

they were alone
so I came

it is cold

we have no heating

I don't know how
we will care
for our cat
and the dog

in the night time
the light
comes
from explosions

that is all

when the sun
comes up
it starts over
again

we are
surrounded
by the sound
of unending gunfire

we are more
afraid
with every breath
we take

if that
is possible . . .

I believe
it is possible

the bath
holds only five litres
now

when that is gone
I think
you can say
goodbye
to maxim

and to his old people

and his cat
and dog

I think
the life that we have
left
is perhaps
this
five litres

dozhd tv (and the search for meaning in swans)

the swans
are dancing
in moscow

I wonder
what does that mean
over there

one by one
the television stations
sign off

this time
the staff said

>   *good night*

>   *good night*
>   *once and*
>   *for all*

the government says
there is no invasion

no war

and the staff
there
at *dozhd* –
tv rain –
must agree

because they said
as they went –
each one –
as they resigned

no

no
to war

while the cygnets
all danced
to tchaikovsky

a beautiful
farewell
and I wonder
just what
it might mean

margot (is at the berlin railway station)

I am the child
of a refugee

she says

my mother –
who is ninety
seven –
fled
from oppressors

in the nineteen
forties

she and I
live now
in germany

ours
is a small place

but
we believe
we have room . . .

enough room
in our unit
to accommodate
more

those people –
poor people –
their husbands
and fathers
are fighting

for *their* home

so
mother
and me

we will take in
another mother
and
her child

history
repeats itself
it seems

and I cannot help
but remember
another time . . .

a long time
ago

when a mother
and her daughter
had need

speaking from russia (in whispers)

no tweets

or twitters

no face-time

no truth
in newspapers
online
or
in hand

don't speak –
no shouting –
just whisper

freedom prevails
in this land

this great land

nobody asked us (in russia)

helping them
is treason
here

isolation
is nothing

everything
will be different
now

this
is the changing
of our world

back
into darkness

do you know . . .

nobody
asked us

that
is the true
pain

knowing
that none
of us
really matter

and to speak
sympathy –
or horror
or sorrow –
for ukraine . . .

that
is a crime

know no peace (in kherson)

I can hear
shelling

every three
or four
minutes

and we cannot leave
kherson
because the enemy
is stopping everyone who moves

checking them

checking their things

their phones

but
we cannot allow them
to believe
they have won

that they have broken
us

so
we march
in the street

there are two
thousand
of us

marching

the enemy
is scared –
they fire their bullets
into the air
to frighten us –
but we are marching
toward them

we will
always
be marching
toward them

they will never
know peace
while ever they stand
in kherson

never before (in warsaw)

*I have been
alive*

*for some years
now*

*I have never seen
anything
like this before*

is he talking
about the war
in ukraine . . .

is he talking
about the fleeing
and their fear . . .

does he speak of
open arms
in poland . . .

is he
referring
to the refugees –
black kenyans
from the ukraine –
now living
in his basement . . .

yes

to all of that

he has never
seen
the like
of these things
before

no corridor (in mariupol)

today
there is no
water
in mariupol

the bathtubs
are empty

there is nothing
to drink

but the corridors
in buildings
that have not
yet
been shelled
are alive

with people
lying down
and people
crying

women
and children
but no food

and no way
to leave

not
without dying

and the corridors –
outside –
the promised roads
to safety
are being blown up
and fired on

there is no place
in mariupol
left
to hide

war is coming to kyiv (just like zminyi island)

they remember
zminyi island
in kyiv

amid all
the preparations
to meet
the invaders

    russian ship
    fuck off

a poster
celebrates
the now famous
retort

while bulldozers
and cranes
re-arrange
the landscape

the war
is coming

the war
is near

the war
is . . .

the very minute
they stop preparing

so they train
with guns
and learn
first-aiding

almost
all of them
are local

to the suburb

to the street

to kyiv

above all
local to kyiv

after
what was done
to kharkiv
they have no doubts

they all belong
to kyiv
and
they must fight

a half a roll of toilet paper (and my own gun)

my name is
ivan

I live
now
in a station

inside the metro

I came to work
a week
ago
and now
I cannot go home

the fighting . . .

it is everywhere

I eat
what the volunteers
bring

I shit
in the station toilets

wipe myself clean
from
a half a roll
of toilet paper

I have a family
out there

a place
I always thought
was my home

they are gone
I think

I did not
get a chance
to say goodbye

you know
I was forty-nine
when we had her

we did not think
that we could

now
she is a child
of war

or even more
its victim

it is
impossible

everything
is impossible

soon –
I think
soon –
I will look
to find
my own gun

bila tserkva is a danger (without pancakes)

maniukina
is sixteen years
old

last night
she made pancakes
until
the explosion

orange light
glass shatters
and shards

there is blood
on her neck

she was lucky

because a boy
on the street
was cut
badly

someone –
her face –
but not badly

not
this time

bila tserkva
is a dangerous place
now

everyone
who can
will soon
leave

it is poland
or
the mountains

or stay to help
in the war

nothing
and nowhere
is safe

and bila tserkva
itself
is a danger

two loaves in kyiv (and the pets to feed)

she tells the story
of her passage
through
shock

and grief

>*I don't cry*
>*all day*
>*any more*
>
>*when I read*
>*the details*
>*of what has happened*
>*overnight*
>*in my homeland*
>
>*bombs*
>*where my father*
>*lives*
>*near kyiv*
>
>*enemy tanks*
>*in small towns –*
>*peaceful places –*
>*I once visited*
>*with friends*
>
>*I*
>*read slowly*
>
>*take a little time*
>*over every sentence*

*allow each one
to settle*

*I make decisions
with each line
of news
about how
I will react*

*my fear
sometimes now
leads me
to stasis*

*a brief paralysis
in which
I can do
nothing*

*until –
eventually –
I reach
for the phone
to make a call*

*to contact family
or friends
who I know
must be near
to the latest explosion*

*to receive
small reassurances
that they survive*

so far

*my mother
spends her time
trying to get food
for her pets*

*herself too –
of course –
but
mainly she worries
for the pets

she told me –
so happily –
on the last day
we spoke

that she had managed
to buy
two loaves
of bread*

all of the left side (of mariupol)

all
of the left side
of the city –
of mariupol –
is burning

everything
is fire
and
there is no water
to put it out

no water
even
to drink

we
are three people
living
in my grandparents
apartment

at least
that
is what we were

now
we are twenty

everyone is running
from the left side
of the city

we
were running
too
but the shelling started
again
just as I had loaded
our little car

so we had to run
back
again

and now
we are twenty
and cats
and dogs

and one parrot

we will try
to leave
again
but . . .

it seems
that ceasefires
are a lie

one side
has no
intention
to stop bombing

call me again

yes
do

I will speak
as long
as I have power
in the battery
of my telephone
but . . .

after today
I am without
hope

I do not know
what
will happen

wedding is the good thing (in a war)

our daughter
is twenty-one

she thought
it was
about time

for we have been
together
since two thousand
and two

both of us
are in
the territorial
defences
and
I hadn't seen him
since the start
of this

so we decided . . .

you know . . .

say the words
tie the knot

we know
now
what tomorrow
may bring
so . . .

anyway
the ceremony
was not
so important

I am just glad
we are both
still
alive
and together

our comrades
believed
we should do more

that such
an occasion
should *be* more

they decided
that we must have
a wedding

that
in the middle
of this war
it would be
a good thing
to have
a wedding

barbarians in tears (at kyiv station)

when our train
stopped
at kyiv station
there were
people
on their knees

begging
to be allowed to squeeze
onto the train

we are –
all of us –
running
for safety

it is what
the enemy wants

we know
that

but
what else
can we do

they are playing
with us
like cats with mice

passage out . . .

no passage out .. . .

    oh sorry
    we blew you up . . .

*oh sorry
you died*

there was
almost
fighting on the platform
to get inside
a carriage

papers waving
everywhere –
birth certificates
passports –
any paper
with your name
to say you are
a genuine ukrainian

they make us
all
into barbarians

and
saying goodbye
to our men
who must stay to fight

I have never seen
so many
tears

from zaporizhzhia to bratislava (to feel a little less afraid)

there is
a little boy
travelling

from zaporizhzhia
to bratislava

his mama
put him on the train

his grandma
waved goodbye

they
could not
travel

and they decided
that
an eleven year old
should have a chance
to live

the enemy
bombing the nuclear plant
is not a good
sign
of things
yet to come

so they packed off
their little boy
while there was still
a window
of time

one more thing . . .

one *less* thing
to be afraid
for

each one should be a flower (in polohovyy budynok)

*place
a rose
for every
baby*

*plant a flower
for every child*

*strew them
wide
in craters
and pools*

*until all
of that country
is wild*

with flowers

~

I wrote –
it wasn't long
ago –
of a maternity hospital
conducting itself
in a basement

I always thought
hospitals
would be . . .

sort of
sacred

but no

you know
how it happened . . .

well
no

I don't suppose you do

there was
a ceasefire . . .

I know
I know

what faith
can you place
in those . . .

anyway
there was
a ceasefire

and then
there was
no hospital

simple
as that

all that is left
is holes
in a wall

like missing teeth

missing mothers

missing babies

just

like

that
~

> *fill*
> *each gap*
> *in the wall*
> *with a plant*
> *that will grow*
>
> *a colour*
> *for each mother*
> *and her child*

changing streets (in vilnius)

vilnius
is changing
street names

that embassy
is now situated on
ukranian heroes
street

just
a small gesture
but
I heard it

vera lytochenko (who is kharkiv's violin) plays a lullaby of basements

she plays
in the basement

a lullaby

to help you
sleep

the big stage
is
a small stage
is all
of the shrunken world

bombs
in the rooftops

bombs
fill the sky

destroy
the earth
up there

so
she plays

solo
on solo

she plays

the audience
are her brothers
and sisters

her audience is
everyone in the world
who can hear

everyone
who can stop themselves
thinking
of the war
for
a moment

she plays
for the sunlight
still streaming above
through the smoke trails
of missiles

and
for me
and
for you

the lullaby
of basements

no boiled eggs for breakfast (in mariupol)

the bombs fall
like rain
onto
what once was
mariupol

if there are
windows left
to tremble
they are shaking

no snow
means
no water
means . . .

a difficult day

there are no
easy
days
in mariupol
anymore

how
do you boil
an egg
without water

how
do you feed
the children

bodies
in the street
are . . .

un-knowable

un-human
and
un-collectible

this is
life now

shells falling
at three
ay-em

no water

bodies
rotten in the streets

and no boiled eggs
for the children
for breakfast

that kyiv (will be gone)

half of kyiv
is in lviv
now

and half
of their husbands
are fighting

it is a war
of separations
in ukraine

they all
want
to go home

all want
to be families
again

but kyiv
is a fortress

each street
a barricade

and the enemy
advances
however slowly

it will end . . .

well

it *will* end

and whatever may be
the kyiv
these people left
will be gone

sleep sweet (in mariupol this is home)

after the bombs
a child
is born

this is not
christmas

there is no
manger

sleep sweet
little one

daddy
and mama
are with you

wherever
you are
you will call
home

why (damir) why

damir
do you recall
I loved you

damir
do you remember
me
at all

how can you
from below
the apartment slide

o
my god

damir
why were you
inside
when the missile
struck

damir . . .

why
at all . . .

just
why

just
why

a little north
of kyiv . . .

why

they do not die no (they are killed)

in chuhuiv
and okhtyrka
it is the children
who die

in buzovo gurivshchyna
as well

mariupol
okhmadit hospital . . .

you know
what I'm getting at

it is not
children
who die . . .

no

they are killed

a stamp (for the zmiinyi)

there is
a new stamp
released
for collectors

a warship
an island
a man

and a finger –
raised jaunty –
into the air

a remembrance
of zmiinyi island

a commemoration
of a moment
and
an attitude

I think I might buy one
though
I am no
collector

it is a remembrance

a commemoration

of those
I
hold brave

maksym and dmytro (who hope to stay lucky)

after five years
in the boy scouts
and
one week
of new instruction . . .

all you've got
is
all you'll get

and you can
consider yourself
a soldier

so leave
the boy behind . . .

just there
beside the door

then
sign
right here

welcome
to the territorials
private maksym

private dmytro

get out there

stay lucky

and
if you do
stay lucky . . .

raise
our national flag
above the kremlin

we hope
that you will both
stay
lucky

picture this in a time of war (take my picture)

picture

a missile
trails smoke
across an orange sky

is it evening?

yes

for some

picture

smoke billows
black
in kharkiv

a resident
is holding her nose
against
the smell
of invasion

picture

some kind
of armoured thing

destroyed

there is
a cage
around the turret

for protection
but
it hasn't worked

picture

a school . . .
or
an office

or
a public building

there is
a mosaic wall
in the background

two women
are preparing
food
for fighting men

and
for fighting
boys

or fighting girls

or grandmothers
and grandpas

picture

wounded men
are being comforted
by
a comrade

they are short
an arm

short
a leg

short
a hope

picture

this one looks
like
the mariupol
maternity hospital

I have seen
those
empty windows
before

picture

cluster bombs
in mykolaiv

picture

firemen

a burning building

no chance
of salvation

picture

the trench-diggers
of kyiv

picture

street food . . .

the *only* food

a saturday bazaar
at knee height

picture

the man
must stay

his child
must go

the train
is almost
ready
to leave

picture

a clown –
according
to his nose –
is interviewing
a little refugee girl

they are
across the border
in moldova

the microphone
is pink
and plastic

an identification badge
suggests
israeli origins

picture

a mummy
in the square
at lviv

they have
wrapped
their culture

head to foot

as bandaged
as some
of the territorials

perhaps soon
it will be
just
as damaged

the sky is burning (oh my god)

oh
my god
 the sky
is turning

red

the colour
of the fire

thirty bombs
and
thirty dead

oh my god

the sky
is raining
fire

oh
my god
they have turned
their guns
on lviv
now

for just
one moment
we thought . . .

but
it doesn't work
like that

oh my god
they mean to raze
us
to the ground

and oh . . .

my god

in lviv
it is raining
fire

today's grief (is for her)

the grief
of today
is for . . .

an unknown

it is true
I know none
yet . . .

even so

even so

her death
raises questions
and feelings
and sorrows

perhaps more

and removes
a little
of the light
from the sun

yes
I think what I feel
is the darkness

closing

breathing my air

I don't know her

did not
know her
but the news
of her passing
is a dark-fisted
blow

and the grief
of today
is
for her

remaining in dnipro (and mykolaiv and cherkasy)

we thought
we would be safer
in dnipro

better –
somehow –
if we were with
our family

we would go
crazy
otherwise

so
even though
the invasion
could be
anytime

we left australia
and came back
to home

~

my mother
is old

how
could I leave her
alone
through all this

I stay
though the missiles
are falling

in mykolaiv
we speak
only ukrainian
now

not long ago
some
spoke russian

it is something –
a small
something –
that brings
me
a little hope

we have each other
through this hardship

~

a young man
and his grandfather
are making
canned meat

for refugees
and
for soldiers

sometimes
they also
make camouflage nets
or
fill sandbags

they defend
by helping
each other

and
by remaining

a long line from beechworth (to kyiv)

from beechworth –
where I live in australia –
the road
travels
south

if I drive
out of town
I will go
past
the golden ball bridge

and
the everton roads –
which
are turn-offs
to the left –
and then
through tarrawingee

that
is twenty-four
k's
and a right hand turn

onto the snow road

wangaratta

is at thirty-eight
k's
but
before that
is a ramp

down
to the freeway

then
we wil be
cruising

on a road
that runs
all the way
to melbourne

but
my imagination
is not going
that far

just
to benalla

that's around about
seventy k's

and three-quarters
of an hour
to drive

I try
but
I can't
picture it

I just
can't picture
those roads
filled
nose-to-tail
for all that distance
by armoured vehicles

with bombs
and missiles

and an intent
to surround my town . . .

my beechworth
or benalla
or wangaratta

my wodonga
or albury
or canberra

it is
beyond me

a failure
of my imagination
to fathom

kyiv digital is an air raid warning (the bomb shelters are wi-fi)

in kyiv
they have a
digital
application –
an app –
that tells you
when
your train will come

where
you can park your car

to let you pay
for your
ticket

a useful
little thing

that lives
on the
telephone

oh

did I mention . . .

it does
air-raids too

the app is working
everywhere
in kyiv

so they changed
the advice
to *missile*

and the *maps*
to *find shelter*

where to locate
your *insulin* supplies

and free *bread*
and
free *water*

all the bomb shelters
now
have wi-fi

a train ticket to lviv (and mental health check) please

there is
a certain
trauma
that comes from being
a child

this world
is not to be taken
lightly

in fact . . .

this world
can be
a net
taker

when you
are young

sometimes
you see it
most
at the train station

at lviv

where the trains
still run
to poland

the station
has psychologists
now

mental health workers

for the mothers
who are distraught
and breaking

and
for the children

who come
catatonic

cannot speak
or react
to things that happen
around them

but draw pictures
of explosion

and the national flag
and
tanks and bombs

and bodies

welcome
to public transport
in ukraine

she dances now (in never land)

olga
danced
the bolshoi

but the steps
became harder
to take

harder
to believe in

so she tiptoed
all the way
to netherlands

never lands

now
she dances
all day
with alexei

and doesn't need
to pirouette
around
her shame

grieving the leaving (from mariupol theatre)

the soft parts
of the auditorium seats –
the parts that you would
sit on
if you were at
a show –
were laid down
end
to end

like that
they served –
you know –
to make
a sort of bed

we had
not enough
of food
for a while

so we fed
only
the children

only
to them

and there was
no gas

no heating

no running water

but
we ended up
making
a sort of
kitchen
in the theatre

and food came –

a little –

there were
perhaps
eight hundred
of us

and for three weeks
we survived
that way

but we knew . . .

all that time
we knew

something terrible
was going
to happen

my family managed
to flee
one day before

anothere group
with four people
already in their car –
and four dogs
and
a cat –
took us

we knew . . .

had
the *feeling*
of something bad
about
to happen

now
we feel
lucky –

and broken inside –
at the same time

you see
we came
to know them

and now
they are gone
while we
are here

I have seen
pictures
of the smoke

and the ruin

and
I grieve

the small soft kindness (of sighetu marmatiei)

the bridge
across the river
tisza

shows the way
from ukraine
to rumania

to a place
named
sighetu marmatiei

it is
a wooden bridge

a venerable
thing
that serves

and *that*
is all it is intended
to do

but
it is lined
now
with colours
and with shapes

with plush
and soft
cloth-noses

for the children
you see

they
are for
the children

who come
in arms
and
with their hands held –
stumbling

who come
with their mothers
and
who come alone

who come
with nothing else
that could
be carried
when they ran
from home

from smoke
and ruin
and noise

explosions
and deaths
and tears

so very many
tears

here
is a toy

here is
a small soft kindness
that a child
can hold

krystina hopes for katriusa (to start over again)

krystyna's little girl
is growing
stronger

each day
stronger . . .

a little more
confident
and vibrant
and alive

but
katriusa asks –
too often
now –
when will we go back
to daddy

when
are we returning
to home

and the hope
is the hope
of a mother

that her child
will forget
all of this

that the day
will come
when they *can* go
back home

to see daddy

and
to start over
again

and she hopes
that her daughter –
that katriusa –
will forget

all of this grief
and pain

stay
a little girl

a child

for as long
as she can

until they can find
her daddy and begin
to live their life
over
again

an audience watches a street full of tanks (at play)

there are tanks
in the streets
in mariupol

where the theatre
is still the site
of a drama

with its sets
underground

while the tanks
are above

all of it
seems a play . . .

the acts
keep unfolding . . .

act two
was a church

then
a hospital

then
a home

the sea
rushes in
where the port
used
to be

the city
is awash
with disasters
that keep playing
to a wide-scattered
audience

some
lie in basements

some
in an office
for planning
(that is moscow

that
is london
and washington)

some
in australia
are trying not
to watch
anymore . . .

and it is proving
a difficult thing

in the drama
that is
mariupol
there is no
city
left

just holes
in the ground
and holes
in the air

and what were
the streets
are tank stations

I wonder
how many
acts
left to play

or when
will it be
intermission

an interval

a break

when will it
be over

at least for
the audience

children are silent, fathers weep, shrapnel lodges (everywhere)

here we are
beside
artum's bed

he holds
a small farm vehicle
tightly
in his hand

he does not speak
anymore

he has shrapnel
embedded
in his belly

and holds
a plastic tractor

~

the blast
caught
masha's leg

where it is
now
she doesn't know

somewhere

she has left
a part
of herself
in mariupol

and does not
speak
a lot
anymore

~

a boy
watched
his mother
die

a death
by fire

he has shrapnel
lodged
inside his skull

but
does not
cry

~

a child
has died

her grandfather
is weeping

her mother
died
beside the little girl

her father
is weeping

all the fathers –
this day –
are weeping

olga feeds the animals (alexander wields his walking stick)

*who else will feed
the animals . . .*

olga
is a volunteer

she is working
at the odesa zoo
alongside
an old man named
alexander

hundreds of people
have run
away
and fear
is everywhere

all their pets . . .

all
the animals

they are all
here
at the zoo

olga
feels the responsibility

there are bears and zebras
and
an elephant

the elephant goes
by the name
of daisy

all of them
all
of them
must be fed
and watered

they must be
calmed

perhaps
it is they
who provide
a little calm
to olga

alexander
wields
his walking stick
as though it were
a gun

love (in zaporizhzhia)

an old car
is . . .

a protective device

women
turn metal
into armour

for their soldier
boys

in zaporizhzhia
they have sewing machines
that will do
that job

the khaki
that will cover steel
is worn
by presidents
while sending out
their
social media

messages
in old car
parts
and olive cloth

~

will body armour
deflect
a slug

turn
a missile
away . . .

no

no

I don't think
that it will

but it will let
a soldier . . .
feel

that all
of the ukraine
is sitting on
his shoulders

what he has
to protect
and
what loves
him

dmytro who died now lives in the lychakiv (and other places)

no one heard
the guns
salute
as they fired
above his grave

no one he knew
was aware
that he
had died

his colleagues
put him in the ground

with a ribbon
for his cross

and the empty
sound
of earth
striking the coffin

dmytro lives

in the lychakiv
in lviv
for evermore

dmytro lives

as a photograph
held
by his mother

dmytro lives

as the spirit
that flies

blue
of the sky
and yellow
of the sun
up above

dmytro lives

even as ukraine
dies

and lives

leaving krasylivka (and the ukraine)

I am preparing
to leave
the ukraine

yet . . .

I am drawn
to return

to look again

~

picture

small housing
in the foreground

shells of high rise
accommodation –
gap-toothed
and destroyed –
haunt
in the middle distance

two people
on a hilltop
gaze –
forlorn –
at the smoke
billowing up
from a missile strike

picture

a tunnel

a basement

the kind
that might serve
as a cool cellar
for wine

or mushroom growing

a handful
of the young
of lviv
are sheltering
from missile blasts
above them

all gazing –
fervently –
at the screens
on their smart phones

news . . .

directions
to greater safety . . .

food
and water . . .

there could be anything

there might
be something

picture

one sits
huddled in a blanket

staring . . .

at nothing

there is nothing
left
to stare at

the other –
wearing a police uniform –
sits
with his head
in his hands

weeping

there is
nothing

~

picture

krasylivka
is a burnt-out car

a dead
tree

a small mountain
of rubble

picture

the view
though fifty-six
windows
is unimpeded

there is no glass
in them

there is
no building
behind

look

see

~

I am leaving . . .

preparing
to leave
the ukraine

but . . .

always

always

there is one
more
picture

the kharkiv humoresque is beautiful (underground)

three violins

one cello

one bass

do you know
bach . . .

orchestral suite
number 3

also
dvorak

the humoresques

about
an hour . . .

a little less

hush now . . .

listen

~

this is the subway
in kharkiv

there will be
no
music-fest
this year

this year of invasion
and
of so much
destruction

later
it will be
a bomb shelter
but . . .

what of that

ukraine
is a land
of culture
and
of sophistication

even underground

~

the last notes
echo

resound

in the aftermath –
after
the music
and
in between
missile strikes –
the silence
is beautiful

they are closing shevchenko's eyes (so he does not have to see)

shevchenko
was a poet
you know

he wrote his verse
in ukrainian

and in ukraine
they named streets
and squares
and universities
in his honour

built statues

a poet

kharkiv's monument
is sixteen metres
tall

and
in that place –
in that
city centre –
he has the extra honour
of a crane

lifting sandbags

surrounding
and engulfing
his rather stern
visage

covering his eyes
to protect him
from what
a poet
should not
have to see

hundreds
upon hundreds
of sandbags

~

the shelling
has been going on
all
through the night

and the morning

the air
is toxic
from fire

a canto a canto (a canto for the ukraine)

    canto
    canto
    canto

mariupol
has died

    canto
    canto
    canto

burned
while
still alive

    canto
    canto
    canto

missiles
in the night

    canto
    canto
    canto

praying

praying

praying
for the light

    ~

kirill

iliya

a little girl
unnamed

a woman –
a body –
with her ankles
tied
together
as neatly
as anyone can do
for the dead
in a time like this . . .

what kind
of time
is this . . .

a tarpaulin
is a shape
that is a body

is a man

quickly
quickly
get them all
into the grave

a solitary grave
to take
so many

cover them
and run

~

>   *canto*
>   *canto*
>   *canto*

kharkiv searches
for her bodies

they lie
here . . .

somewhere
just a little
below

>   *canto*
>   *canto*
>   *canto*

long ice
descends
to place
a kiss
upon the snow

>   *canto*
>   *canto*
>   *canto*

the city
was . . .

is

completely gone

>   *canto*
>   *canto*
>   *canto*

and the metro –
underground –
is all . . .

to call
a *home*

~

    the situation
    here
    is
    very bad . . .

    we are
    terrorised
    by shelling

    dozens

    dozens
    have been killed

    we have
    no medicine

    we have
    no more food

    we have no water
    any more

    we do
    our best

    all of us

    we do
    our best

*but every day
is another asking:*

*what did we do
to deserve
to be so
forsaken*

~

    *canto
    canto
    canto*

kyiv
is still a place
of safety

    *canto
    canto
    canto*

kyiv
will hold on
with all its life

    *canto
    canto
    canto*

until
the missiles
strike it down

    *canto
    canto
    canto*

oh why
must good things
always
die

always die

~

yuri lives
on the thirteenth floor

his building is
untouched
in the heart
of kyiv

his family
have fled
to sweden
with his blessing

he remains
as a man
of age
to take up arms
in the territorial
army

he believes the war
is because of the enemy's
hatred

citizens
on the street
are waiting –
holding their
metaphorical
breath –

for the catastrophe
is surely near

it is coming

and yet . . .

>   *and yet*
>   *if we can get*
>   *our hands*
>   *on food*
>
>   *on water*
>
>   *and yet*
>   *while we breathe*
>   *we can cling*
>   *to life*
>
>   *and yet*
>   *and so*
>   *we somehow*
>   *get used to it*
>
>   *a new kind*
>   *of normal*
>   *until . . .*

the next missile screams
and shrills
and falls

too close

and then
another somebody
dies

from odesa to kyiv the little world (is shrinking)

picture

it is a camp

bedding
and baggage

tramp people

> *pillars*
> *to mark out*
> *domiciles*
>
> *clear-paths*
> *down the centre aisle*
>
> *amenities*
> *lost in the distance*
>
> *trains*
> *on either side*

it is the kharkiv
subway

picture

for a long time
I cannot see
the cat

against the blue
of a railway carriage
and the purple hue
of a suitcase

it is –
I think –
part-cheshire

picture

a man
sits
right on the edge
of the platform

almost
his rear
above the rails

old

he looks
old

but
he may not be

everyone
looks older
since february

picture

halyna
looks up
at the sky

through a hole
in her roof

the sun
appears to be shining

picture

a grand princess

a priest
or shepherd
with a crook
in his hands

one other . . .

all
being sandbagged
in kyiv

picture

a young woman
smokes

dwarfed
by surrounding
sandbags
outside the volunteer centre
in mykolaiv

the young man
beside her
holds his head
in his hands

despair
is never far

a cigarette
helps

picture

goodbye
goodbye

a kiss
before leaving . . .

the train
will wave
odesa
goodbye

goodbye

the accommodations made by dracao and cat (but not the dog)

dracoa
is a white ferret

it is not
true
to say that he
and the cat-
named *cat* –
are friends
but . . .

the dog
that lives across the platform
hates
both of them
so

the friend
of my enemy . . .

well

this could be
home
for a long time

it has already
gone a month
by now

deep underground
in the kharkiv
railway station
accommodations
must
be made

the truth of time (as revealed by the pictures)

picture 1

a group
of soldiers
are hanging out
of the doors
and windows
of a moving train

they are leaving
egypt

heading
to the western front

ready
for a stoush

a bit
of a barney

it's about time
to come to grips
with the enemy

they
are cherry ripe
for a bit
of a blue

picture 2

dimitriy
is holding olga

so tight
there is no
space
between them
on the platform

a blue train
with yellow trim
is nearly ready

she
will go
to poland
across the border

dimitriy
will join
his friends
in the territorials

one week
to train

to hold a rifle
and learn
first aid

then away

he must forget
to be an accountant

he is a front-line fighter
now

picture 3

a heap of rubble –
of bricks
and half-bricks

of timber and concrete
and dust –
lies as a mound

among mounds

it is
a streetscape

an avenue
of homes

destroyed by artillery
thrown
from a distance
by a brave enemy
who didn't know
or
didn't care

an AIF soldier
rifle
slung over a shoulder
picks his way
toward camera

there is nothing left
that might hold
use
or meaning

picture 4

a village
near kyiv
is a series
of mounds

rubble
that was homes
and houses
a month or so
ago

a woman
is sifting

searching
for something –
anything –
that might
have a use

destroyed
by missiles and artillery
thrown
from a long way off

by an enemy
who didn't know . . .

didn't care

she hasn't found
a lot
that will be useful

picture 5

the ambulance corps
is one man short

a couple of the boys
are standing
around
a mounded grave

taking pictures
of
a wooden cross

he was a corporal
from castlemaine

a bearer

a good man

and the folk back home
surely
are going to grieve

but . . .

meanwhile

they need another man
to bear one end
of a stretcher

picture 6

the funeral
is a full ceremony

orthodox

open casket
with the body
concealed
by a gauze cloth

his mother
is draped
across the coffin

weeping

women
in the gathering
are shedding tears
as well

men
are looking
into the middle distance
or
at their
rifles

contemplating

he was a solicitor
until
a couple of weeks back

one less
to fight
with the territorials

~

pictures
pictures
they will not
let me sleep
in the night

they shout at me
that we have come
full circle

and in the ukraine
it is 1916
again

Sources

1. lullaby (for lviv): Harriet Alexander, The Daily Mail (UK) https://www.dailymail.co.uk/news/article-10566995/Ukrainian-woman-shows-Molotov-cocktails-finding-recipe-Google.html
2. right now (we are kyiv): Ukraine crisis live, The Guardian hhttps://www.theguardian.com/world/live/2022/feb/27/russia-ukraine-latest-news-missile-strikes-on-oil-facilities-reported-as-some-russian-banks-cut-off-from-swift-system-live
3. anastasia and tatiana (moscva is too close): Steve Cannane, The ABC (Australia) https://www.abc.net.au/news/2022-02-28/inside-the-resistance-to-vladimir-putin-s-invasion-of-ukraine/100866594
4. holding vlado (close): No reference.
5. back into the (snake) water: ABC/Reuters, The ABC (Australia) https://www.abc.net.au/news/2022-02-28/ukraine-border-guard-snake-island-russia-attack/100867150
6. fallen (quietly weeping): Spencer Bokat-Lindell, New York Times https://www.nytimes.com/2022/03/02/opinion/ukraine-putin-nuclear-war.htm
7. the blue and yellow blood (of the deputy mayor of kakhovka): Euromaidan Press https://mobile.twitter.com/EuromaidanPress/status/1497945980968136709
8. the metro (is also home): Jessica Riga, Jacqueline Howard, Nick Sas, and Paul Johnson, ABC (Australia) https://www.abc.net.au/news/2022-03-01/ukraine-russia-invasion-war-kyiv-kharkiv/100870192
9. vasylkiv (is fighting on): Shaun Walker, The Guardian https://www.theguardian.com/world/2022/feb/28/vasylkiv-why-this-small-ukrainian-town-is-now-a-big-russian-target
10. god knows (volyn and rivne): Ukraine crisis live, The Guardian https://www.theguardian.com/world/live/2022/feb/28/russia-ukraine-war-latest-news-update-conflict-belarus-putin-nuclear-deterrence-order-kyiv-russian-invasion-live-updates
11. in okhtyrka (the tsentral'ne): Peter Beaumont, Luke Harding, Jon Henley, Julian Borger, and Dan Sabbagh, The Guardian https://www.theguardian.com/world/2022/mar/01/fears-of-bloody-fight-for-kyiv-as-huge-russian-army-convoy-gathers-on-outskirts
12. tears in the storm-water system (are kharkiv's blood): Joel Gunter, The BBC https://www.bbc.com/news/world-europe-60579247
13. the glory (of the national digital library of ukraine): Nick Poole https://twitter.com/NickPoole1/status/1498387510078185477
14. ants with one heart (one home): Luke Harding, The Guardian https://www.theguardian.com/world/2022/mar/02/ukrainian-volunteers-united-front-against-russia-invasion
15. oleg (kherson is falling): Alexandra Topping and Hibaq Farah, The Guardian https://www.theguardian.com/world/2022/mar/02/ukraine-police-officers-entire-family-killed-while-fleeing-russian-invasion
16. moscow children (are very very wise): Nadeem Badshah, The Guardian https://www.theguardian.com/world/2022/mar/02/moscow-police-arrest-children-for-laying-flowers-at-ukrainian-embassy
17. kyiv gives birth (in its basements): Guardian News, YouTube https://youtu.be/bK58edIjiK8 take another tank (for the motherland): Staff and agencies (Reuters) The Guardian https://www.theguardian.com/world/2022/mar/03/ukraine-authorities-say-seized-russian-tanks-dont-need-to-be-declared-on-tax-form

18. a search for solace (for a champion): ABC/wires, ABC (Australia) https://www.abc.net.au/news/2022-03-04/ukrainian-woman-plays-we-are-the-champions-at-polish-border/100880988
19. there will be a party soon (in the kyiv forest): Orla Guerin, BBC https://www.bbc.com/news/world-europe-60607649
20. after maxim's five litres (say goodbye): Joel Gunter, The BBC https://www.bbc.com/news/world-europe-60601235
21. dozhd tv (and the search for meaning in swans): Edwina Seselja, ABC (Australia) https://www.abc.net.au/news/2022-03-04/swan-lake-broadcast-signals-turmoil-in-russia/100881424
22. margot (is at the berlin railway station): Damian Grammaticas, BBC https://www.bbc.com/news/world-europe-60611188
23. speaking from russia (in whispers): Eilish Hart https://twitter.com/EilishHart/status/1499831806807494663/photo/1
24. nobody asked us (in russia): Simon Fraser, BBC https://www.bbc.com/news/world-europe-60585720
25. know no peace (in kherson): Russia-Ukraine War, BBC https://www.bbc.com/news/world-europe-60632587
26. never before (in warsaw): Lorenzo Tondo in Lublin and Weronika Strzyżyńska , The Guardian https://www.theguardian.com/global-development/2022/mar/05/poland-rush-to-aid-ukraine-refugees-russia-war
27. no corridor (in mariupol): Ukraine crisis live , The Guardian https://www.theguardian.com/world/live/2022/mar/05/russia-ukraine-war-latest-news-nato-gives-green-light-to-bombing-with-lack-of-no-fly-zone-says-zelenskiy
28. war is coming to kyiv (just like zminyi island): Shaun Walker, The Guardian https://www.theguardian.com/world/2022/mar/05/fortress-kyiv-ukraine-grimly-anticipates-russia-advance
29. a half a roll of toilet paper (and my own gun): Shaun Walker, The Guardian https://www.theguardian.com/world/2022/mar/05/fortress-kyiv-ukraine-grimly-anticipates-russia-advance
30. bila tserkva is a danger (without pancakes): Loveday Morris, The Washington Post https://www.washingtonpost.com/world/2022/03/05/ukraine-russia-kyiv-bila-tserkva/?utm_source=rss&utm_medium=referral&utm_campaign=wp_world
31. two loaves in kyiv (and the pets to feed): Marta Shokalo, BBC https://www.bbc.com/news/world-europe-60633888
32. all of the left side (of mariupol): Joel Gunter, BBC https://www.bbc.com/news/world-europe-60637338
33. wedding is the good thing (in a war): Associated Press, ABC (Australia) https://www.abc.net.au/news/2022-03-07/ukrainian-defence-fighters-marry-in-frontline-wedding/100888214
34. barbarians in tears (at kyiv station): Joel Gunter, BBC https://www.bbc.com/news/world-europe-60645126
35. from zaporizhzhia to bratislava (to feel a little less afraid): Russia-Ukraine War, BBC https://www.bbc.com/news/world-europe-60659365
36. each one should be a flower (in polohovyy budynok): BBC News Channel, BBC https://www.bbc.com/news/live/world-europe-60657155 and Reuters, ABC (Australia) https://www.abc.net.au/news/2022-03-10/ukrainian-officials-say-russian-air-strike-hit-mariupol-hospital/100897362

37. changing streets (in vilnius): Agence France-Presse, The Guardian https://www.theguardian.com/world/2022/mar/10/lithuania-names-road-leading-to-russian-embassy-ukrainian-heroes-street
38. vera (who is kharkiv's violin) plays a lullaby of basements: Associated Press, The Guardian https://www.theguardian.com/world/2022/mar/09/ukraines-cellar-violinist-plays-over-the-bombs
39. no boiled eggs for breakfast (in Mariupol): Luke Harding and Caroline Bannock, The Guardian https://www.theguardian.com/world/2022/mar/10/not-scared-tired-conditions-mariupol-siege-medieval-ukraine
40. that kyiv (will be gone): Lorenzo Tondo, The Guardian https://www.theguardian.com/news/2022/mar/10/we-all-want-to-return-residents-fleeing-kyiv-mourn-a-deserted-city
41. sleep sweet (in mariupol this is home) Kaamil Ahmed, The Guardian https://www.theguardian.com/world/2022/mar/11/ukraine-woman-who-escaped-mariupol-maternity-ward-gives-birth
42. they do not die no (they are killed): Iryna Venediktova, Twitter https://twitter.com/VenediktovaIV/status/1502567437102891009?ref_src=twsrc%5Etfw%7Ctwcamp%5Etweetembed%7Ctwterm%5E1502567437102891009%7Ctwgr%5E%7Ctwcon%5Es1_&ref_url=https%3A%2F%2Fwww.theguardian.com%2Fworld%2Flive%2F2022%2Fmar%2F12%2Fukraine-news-russia-war-ceasefire-broken-humanitarian-corridors-kyiv-russian-invasion-live-vladimir-putin-volodymyr-zelenskiy-latest-updates-live
43. a stamp (for the zmiinyi): Chris Michael, The Guardian https://www.theguardian.com/world/2022/mar/12/ukraine-reveals-russian-warship-go-fuck-yourself-postage-stamp
44. picture this in a time of war (take my picture): Pictures of war, BBC https://www.bbc.com/news/world-europe-60720169
45. the sky is burning (oh my god): Hugo Bachega BBC https://www.bbc.com/news/world-europe-60728208
46. today's grief (is for her): Associated Press in Mariupol ,The Guardian https://www.theguardian.com/world/2022/mar/14/mariupol-ukraine-hospital-bombed-woman-baby-die
47. remaining in dnipro (and mykolaiv and cherkasy): Joshua Boscaini, Dubravka Voloder and Jenny Cai ABC (Australia) https://www.abc.net.au/news/2022-03-13/why-these-people-stay-in-ukraine-russian-invasion-war/100902036
48. a long line from beechworth (to kyiv): Alba Sanz, Atalayar https://atalayar.com/en/content/60-kilometre-russian-military-convoy-heads-kiev
49. kyiv digital is an air raid warning (the bomb shelters are wi-fi): Isobel Koshiw and Lisa O'Carroll, The Guardian https://www.theguardian.com/world/2022/mar/15/kyiv-transport-app-is-transformed-into-life-saving-war-information-tool
50. a train ticket to lviv (and mental health check) please: Lorenzo Tondo, The Guardian https://www.theguardian.com/global-development/2022/mar/15/ukraine-child-mental-health-crisis
51. she dances now (in never land): AFP, https://www.abc.net.au/news/2022-03-17/ballerina-olga-smirnova-quits-bolshoi-ballet-over-ukraine-war/100916824
52. grieving the leaving (from mariupol theatre): Hugo Bachega & Orysia Khimiak, BBC https://www.bbc.com/news/world-europe-60776929

53. the small soft kindness (of sighetu marmatiei): Andrei Chirileasa, https://www.romania-insider.com/romania-photo-toys-bridge-sighetu-marmatiei-ukrainian-refugees
54. krystina hopes for katriusa (to start over again): Dan Johnson, BBC https://www.bbc.com/news/av/world-europe-60794423
55. an audience watches a street full of tanks (at play): Hugo Bachega, BBC https://www.bbc.com/news/world-europe-60806973
56. children are silent, fathers weep, shrapnel lodges (everywhere): Wyre Davies, BBC https://www.bbc.com/news/world-europe-60814913
57. olga feeds the animals (alexander wields his walking stick): Andrew Harding BBC https://www.bbc.com/news/world-europe-60785791
58. love (in zaporizhzhia): Ukraine crisis live, The Guardian https://www.theguardian.com/world/live/2022/mar/22/russia-ukraine-war-zelenskiy-urges-talks-with-putin-biden-flags-clear-sign-russia-considering-chemical-weapons-live
59. dmytro who died now lives in the lychakiv (and other places): Joel Gunter, BBC https://www.bbc.com/news/world-europe-60801586
60. leaving krasylivka (and the ukraine): Ukraine crisis live, The Guardian https://www.theguardian.com/world/live/2022/mar/26/russia-ukraine-war-zelenskiy-hails-powerful-blows-by-ukrainian-army-as-russia-hints-at-scaling-back-offensive-live
61. the kharkiv humoresque is beautiful (underground): Live Updates, Al Jazeera https://www.aljazeera.com/news/2022/3/26/ukraine-war-strategic-failure-for-russia-biden-liveblog
62. they are closing shevchenko's eyes (so he does not have to see): Assed Baig, Al Jazeera https://www.aljazeera.com/news/2022/3/26/ukraine-war-strategic-failure-for-russia-biden-liveblog
63. a canto a canto (a canto for the ukraine)
    - 'Why? Why? Why?' descends into despair, Mstyslav Chernov, Evgeniy Maloletka and Lori Hinnant, AP News https://apnews.com/article/russia-ukraine-war-mariupol-descends-into-despair-708cb8f4a171ce3f1c1b0b8d090e38e3
    - The Devastation of Kharkiv, Ukraine, Masha Gessen, The New Yorker https://www.newyorker.com/culture/photo-booth/the-devastation-of-kharkiv
    - From Lviv to Kyiv, snapshots of Ukraine in a time of war, David Gormezano, France24 https://www.france24.com/en/europe/20220324-from-lviv-to-kyiv-snapshots-of-ukraine-in-a-time-of-war from odesa to kyiv the little world (is shrinking): Ukraine crisis live, The Guardian https://www.theguardian.com/world/live/2022/mar/28/russia-ukraine-war-latest-news-zelenskiy-putin-live-updates
64. the accommodations made by dracao and cat (but not the dog): Emma Graham-Harrison, The Guardian https://www.theguardian.com/world/2022/mar/29/kharkiv-ukraine-underground-refuge-life

the truth of time (as revealed by the pictures): No reference.

Author Information

About the Author

Frank Prem has been a storytelling poet since his teenage years. He has been a psychiatric nurse through all of his professional career, which now exceeds forty years.

He has been published in magazines, online zines, and anthologies in Australia, and in a number of other countries, and has both performed and recorded his work as spoken word.

He lives with his wife in the beautiful township of Beechworth in North East Victoria, Australia.

Connect with Frank

As the author, I hope you enjoyed this volume of poetry collection. I think that mine is a unique style of writing that can appeal well beyond a *'pure poetry'* readership.

If you enjoyed it, I'd like to ask you to do two small things for me.

First, take a moment to find your favourite online retail store and leave a short review of the book in your preferred store.

Online reviews provide social proof to readers and are critical to Indie authors such as myself.

The second thing is, please pop over to my author page **www.FrankPrem.com**, and subscribe to receive my occasional Newsletter.

From time to time I'll let you know what is happening with myself and my writing, as well as keeping you informed of any giveaways I may be planning.

You can also find me on Facebook and Twitter.

Other Published Works

Free Verse Poetry

Small Town Kid (2018)

Devils In The Wind (2019)

The New Asylum (2019)

Herja, Devastation - With Cage Dunn (2019)

Walk Away Silver Heart (2020)

A Kiss for the Worthy (2020)

Rescue and Redemption (2020)

Pebbles to Poems (2020)

The Garden Black (2022)

A Specialist at The Recycled Heart (2022)

Picture Poetry/Spoken Image

Voices (In The Trash) (2020)

The Beechworth Bakery Bears (2021)

Sheep On The Somme (2021)

Waiting For Frank-Bear (2021)

A Lake Sambell Walk (2021)

What Readers Say

Small Town Kid

A modern-day minstrel Small-Town Kid is a wonderful collection —S. T. (Australia)

A poet's walk through his childhood in a small Australian town.—J. L. (USA)

Devil In The Wind

Instantly grips you by the throat in his step-by-step story of survival. Bravo! —K. K. (USA)

Outstanding! —B. T. (Australia)

The New Asylum

Words can't do justice to the emotional journey I travelled. __C. D. (Australia)

If I had to pick one book over the past year that has truly resonated with me, this would be it. __K. B. (USA)

Walk Away Silver Heart

Has an extraordinary way with words. — R C (United States)

As Memorable as My Favorite Music — M D (United States)

A Kiss For The Worthy

A Celebration of Life Written in Thoughtful Bursts of Poetic Expression — M C (United States)

With every verse, I found myself reflecting about myself, my life, and the world —K

Rescue and Redemption

The passion of love in its many forms explored by one for another.—J L (United States)

I've enjoyed every word, every breath. Every moment within the life of these stories.—C D (Australia)

Herja, Devastation

Refreshingly original. Highly recommended! —G. B. (Australia)

Index of Individual Poems

A

a canto a canto (a canto for the ukraine) 140
after maxim's five liters (say goodbye) 44
a half a roll of toilet paper (and my own gun) 62
all of the left side (of mariupol) 69
a long line from beechworth (to kyiv) 106
a lullaby (for lviv) 7
anastasia and tatiana (moscva is too close) 13
an audience watches a street full of tanks (at play) 121
ants with one heart (one home) 33
a search for solace (for a champion) 40
a stamp (for the zmiinyi) 91
a train ticket to lviv (and mental health check) please 111

B

back into the (snake) water 16
barbarians in tears (at kyiv station) 74
bila tserkva is a danger (without pancakes) 64

C

changing streets (in vilnius) 81
children are silent, fathers weep, shrapnel lodges (everywhere) 124

D

dozhd tv (and the search for meaning in swans) 47

E

each one should be a flower (in polohovyy budynok) 78

F

fallen (quietly weeping) 17
from odesa to kyiv the little world (is shrinking) 147
from zaporizhzhia to bratislava (to feel a little less afraid) 76

G

god knows (volyn and rivne) 27
grieving the leaving (from mariupol theatre) 114

H

holding vlado (close) 15

I

in okhtyrka (the tsentral'ne) 28

K

know no peace (in kherson) 54
krystina hopes for katriusa (to start over again) 119
kyiv digital is an air raid warning (the bomb shelters are wi-fi) 109
kyiv gives birth (in its basements) 37

L

leaving krasylivka (and the ukraine) 132
love (in zaporizhzhia) 128

M

maksym and dmytro (who hope to stay lucky) 92
margot (is at the berlin railway station) 49
moscow children (are very very wise) 36

N

never before (in warsaw) 56
nobody asked us (in russia) 52
no boiled eggs for breakfast (in mariupol) 84
no corridor (in mariupol) 58

O

olga feeds the animals (alexander wields his walking stick) 126
o oleg (kherson is falling) 35

P

picture this in a time of war (take my picture) 94

R

remaining in dnipro (and mykolaiv and cherkasy) 103
right now (we are kyiv) 11

S

she dances now (in never land) 113
sleep sweet (in mariupol this is home) 88
speaking from russia (in whispers) 51

T

take another tank (for the motherland) 38
tears in the storm-water system (are kharkiv's blood) 30
that kyiv (will be gone) 86
the accommodations made by dracao and cat (but not the dog) 151
the glory (of the national digital library of ukraine) 31
the kharkiv humoresque is beautiful (underground) 136
the metro (is also home) 22
there will be a party soon (in the kyiv forest) 42
the sky is burning (oh my god) 99

the small soft kindness (of sighetu marmatiei) 117
the truth of time (as revealed by the pictures) 152
they are closing shevchenko's eyes (so he does not have to see) 138
they do not die no (they are killed) 90
today's grief (is for her) 101
two loaves in kyiv (and the pets to feed) 66

V

vasylkiv (is fighting on) 24
vera lytochenko (who is kharkiv's violin) plays a lullaby of basements 82

W

war is coming to kyiv (just like zminyi island) 60
wedding is the good thing (in a war) 72
why (damir) why 89

www.FrankPrem.com